An
UNSTUCK
Christmas
Devotional

A quiet time
A reflective response
An Intentional journey to the manger

Pat Layton

Join us in The Unstuck Woman Club on Facebook for ongoing LIFE UNSTUCK fun and friendships!

Table of Contents

Greetings Friend,

Welcome to An Unstuck Christmas Devotional!

Can I get a whoot—whoot?!

I love this sweet gathering of women walking together through the Love Letter found in Luke Chapters 1 and 2. This Christmas we even add a bit of fun and frivolity to our Christmas Holidays.

Every year we gather, we anticipate our intentional time of quiet reflection with unrestrained glee. I KNOW who you are!! I am always praying and planning reasons for us to get together. I have likely met you on Facebook or via my monthly e-letters. I may have hugged your neck at an event or virtually ministered beside you through my book *Life Unstuck* or *Surrendering the Secret*, my abortion recovery study.

Maybe—we are just now meeting for the first time. If so, get ready, we will become life-long friends and sisters in Christ!

These devotions came straight from my personal prayer journals and are ready to be gently mixed with your own. The season that heightens on Thanksgiving and calms on Christmas Day is truly to be treasured. By using this devotional tool together, we have made an INTENTIONAL CHOICE to keep our Christmas UNSTUCK and free, allowing us to BE and RECEIVE some special BLESSINGS!

My suggestion is that you use the pages provided each day for your personal devotions in the "YOUR HEART" space provided.

Every Christmas season is different so be sure to use this FRESH VERSION for a FRESH look into the birth of Jesus.

To enhance our time together **we will be meeting as a reading group** via **The Unstuck Woman Club on Facebook and on my website blog for more personal interaction and to share ideas with other women!** I will be giving away TONS of FREE PRIZES and gifts to sparkle up our dialog over Christmas as we go.

I am always excited to hear YOUR Heart as I share MY HEART with you.

Let's get started, shall we?

We will be starting on December One in Luke Chapter One and hang out there together for the next 25 days.

I am thankful for you!

Pat

DAY 1   Luke 1:1-4 (NIV)

Many have undertaken to draw up an account of the things that have been fulfilled[a] among us, 2 just as they were handed down to us by those who from the first were eyewitnesses and servants of the word. 3 With this in mind, since I myself have carefully investigated everything from the beginning, I too decided to write an orderly account for you, most excellent Theophilus, 4 so that you may know the certainty of the things you have been taught.

MY HEART

Whenever I drag the heavy plastic bin that holds thirty plus years' worth of my old prayer journals from under my bed, blow the layer of dust off the top and crack open the lid, my HEART does that funny dance between terror and delight. You may know the feeling; It's like what happens when you ride Space Mountain at Disney for the first time. My mind always reviews my options - burn these and let all this "stuff" stay between me and Jesus OR keep saving them as a raw record of "the things that have been fulfilled...so that you may know."

Memories hold such a personal place. My family always teases me about the stories I share in my books and my speeches. They always remember things differently than I do. The truth is likely somewhere in the middle.

In these familiar verses Dr. Luke, the author of this book of the Bible, goes on record with his version of the birth and infancy of Jesus as it was handed down to him. This is the longest book of the Gospels and is essentially written from Mary's perspective. Dr. Luke was a student of truth and details and presents a beautiful narrative of, not only the birth of Jesus, but his boyhood and launch into ministry. Luke introduces Jesus as "The Son of Man" and shares His prayer life, healing touch and His compassion for the lost and hurting. My hope with Quest to An Unstuck Christmas is that we take a FRESH and RENEWED look at these very familiar passages. Let's get started, shall we?!

Prayer: Father, thank you for leading me to this special journey with you during this holiday season. I trust you for the time and the space to get quiet and reflect upon your birth in my life. Show me some NEW things, Lord. Things that I have never seen. Most of all, I want to see you in a fresh way today. Open my eyes, Lord. I want to see Jesus. Amen!

YOUR HEART

_____

_____

_____

_____

_____

_____

_____

_____

_____

_____

_____

_____

_____

_____

_____

_____

_____

_____

_____

_____

_____

_____

_____

DAY 2   Luke 1:5-7 (NIV)

In the time of Herod King of Judea there was a priest named Zechariah, who belonged to the priestly division of Abijah; his wife Elizabeth was also a descendant of Aaron. 6 Both of them were righteous in the sight of God, observing all the Lord's commands and decrees blamelessly. 7 But they were childless because Elizabeth was not able to conceive, and they were both very old.

MY HEART

In today's verses our storyteller, Dr. Luke, sets us up for the main drama by sharing some extenuating, yet critical, circumstances of the drama. As a writer, I have been taught that a great book chapter starts with an "anchor story" that gets you at "Hello." One that is personal, descriptive and invites the reader into the scene. Dr. Luke mastered that step by starting his story of the birth of Jesus with the side story of relatives in crisis who would return to our story again and again.

Today's verses share some extended family pain and loss. We learn about Elizabeth's desire for a child, the sweet but cumbersome appeal of her priestly husband, Zechariah, and the first miracle in a long line of miracles.

We all have family drama, do we not?

The Holidays often set us up for engagement that may have been avoided all year, if not all YEARS! There is the bickering Aunt and Uncle. The cousin who drinks too much or is so loud the neighbors ask questions about your dinner conversation for weeks. There might be the cousin whose undisciplined children wildly take over your home at

Thanksgiving and, in spite of your putting away the valuables, pulls the bathroom sink off the wall.

You get my drift :)

Through Dr. Luke's story we find these particular extended family members of Jesus to be "upright in the sight of God" yet a bit doubtful when it comes right down to believing for an all-out miracle. Is there a miracle needed anywhere in your life today? In your own home or one of a family member? I can list several as I write. As I consider family and friends who will gather again over the next few weeks to celebrate family, acknowledge and embrace the birth of Jesus and prepare their hearts and dreams for a New Year, I can think of many needed miracles.

We need to see a marriage saved.

We need some addictions healed.

We need some forgiveness finalized.

We need SEVERAL healing miracles!

Let's apply today's focus and prayers to those in our family who need the kind of miracle that Zechariah and Elizabeth experienced and then let's get our "testimony of praise" on track, from unbelief to trust.

Together. Today.

Let's believe God, shall we?

Prayer: Lord, show me those family members and friends you have supernaturally planned for my life before time began. You do not make mistakes! ALL of your plan works together. Every little piece. Bring them to my mind often today as I speak UNSTUCK FAITH over them and trust that you will complete your work in their lives. Show me MY PART, Lord. Is it a word of hope? Is it a chicken casserole? Is it an invitation to my church? Is it a kind errand to release their burdens? Open my eyes, Lord. I want to see you today. Amen.

YOUR HEART

_____

_____

_____

_____

_____

_____

_____

_____

_____

_____

_____

_____

_____

_____

_____

_____

_____

_____

_____

_____

_____

_____

DAY 3   Luke 1:11-17 (NIV)

11 Then an angel of the Lord appeared to him, standing at the right side of the altar of incense.12 When Zechariah saw him, he was startled and was gripped with fear.13 But the angel said to him: "Do not be afraid, Zechariah; your prayer has been heard. Your wife Elizabeth will bear you a son, and you are to call him John." 14 He will be a joy and delight to you, and many will rejoice because of his birth,15 for he will be great in the sight of the Lord. He is never to take wine or other fermented drink, and he will be filled with the Holy Spirit even before he is born.16 He will bring back many of the people of Israel to the Lord their God.17 And he will go on before the Lord, in the spirit and power of Elijah to turn the hearts of the parents to their children and the disobedient to the wisdom of the righteous - to make ready a people prepared for the Lord."

MY HEART

How many times does this verse refer to fear or dread?

How many times is joy the focus?

Is this a familiar reverberation in your life?

We have seen that Zechariah was a man whom we have already identified as "upright, obedient to God's laws, a man who was chosen to serve as a 'Priest' before the Lord."

Although I cannot imagine the honor of being described the way Zechariah was, I do relate to many occurrences in this scene.

For example, I am certain I would be "gripped by fear," regardless of the level of my faith or my beliefs, if an

ANGEL appeared before me in the middle of my prayer time!

Also, sometimes, even when I have a long list of the needs of others in front of me, I get distracted by my own needs and, like Zechariah, begin losing my focus. How about you, friend? Can you relate to times of prayer that end up as time of pout?

God is good, all the time! The first thing the angel Gabriel said to him is, "Your prayer has been heard," and, "Your wife will bear a son." THAT would be cool, wouldn't it? As words of your prayer are uttered, an ANGEL speaks up and says, "YES! Granted!"

YUM!

I don't know about you, but as we enter into these last days until Christmas, I have some unanswered prayers. I have some unmet desires. I'm betting you do as well.

How about for the next few days we put those needs aside and "serve as priest" on behalf of our family and friends. Let's lay aside, just for a few days, our own burdens, desires and unmet expectations.

Secondly, let's decide NOT to be startled by God's presence but rather to EXPECT it. Let's choose to believe and not doubt. Just for today :)

Prayer: Lord, thank you for ALWAYS hearing my prayers. You know what I need when I need it. You meet me when I pray, wherever I pray. Thank you that your Word instructs us that your ANGELS have charge over me and my family. At my command, they are assigned to guard and protect us. Help me to keep my eyes on you, Lord. I am bringing my needs and the needs of my family to your throne today, Lord. Help me to trust and depend upon you and most of all TO WATCH FOR YOU TODAY! Amen.

YOUR HEART

_____

_____

_____

_____

_____

_____

_____

_____

_____

_____

_____

_____

_____

_____

_____

_____

_____

_____

_____

_____

_____

_____

_____

_____

_____

DAY 4   Luke 1:18 (NIV)

Zechariah asked the angel, "How can I be sure of this? I am an old man and my wife is well along in years."

MY HEART

We have all been guilty of Zechariah's lack of faith at some point or another.

We have all grown weary in the wait. We have all looked around at the circumstances and said (or at least THOUGHT): "Are you seein' what I'm seein', Lord?" The Word that God spoke to my heart this morning as I tried to move on to the next verse was this – It is not only lack of our own faith that causes doubt, it is the LIE of LIMITATIONS. Let's face it, friend. We DO, in fact, have limitations. Frankly, getting older is a huge one in my mirror every day. Most of the dreams I have are dreams of a 30-40 something. Unlike Zachariah, I forget I am old!

I often ask God, "How can I be sure of....?" God always says back---"My love, my power, my plans for you are limitless!" If you are in a place of questioning "how can I be sure...?" or placing limits on God's power in your heart, your mind or your mouth, then today is the day to surrender.

It's no coincidence that Gabriel shut Zechariah's mouth!! Our mouths can be a hot bed of trouble, a noteworthy issue I share more about in my book Life Unstuck. Today, God has refreshed my heart about the topic. Speaking UNBELIEF creates unbelief both in our own hearts and the heart of others. What we hear, we rehearse. Let's take this season of enjoying an UNSTUCK CHRISTMAS to change what we say and say what we PRAY! I believe God can and God will!!

Prayer: Lord, thank you for reminding me when I need to be reminded that the words of my mouth along with the meditations of my heart are meant to be pleasing to you. I want them to be pleasing to you. Show me today, Lord, where is my unbelief? Where am I doubting you? Lead me to confession, repentance and change! Help me to speak only what YOU say and to overflow faith to those around me!

YOUR HEART

_____

_____

_____

_____

_____

_____

_____

_____

_____

_____

_____

_____

_____

_____

_____

_____

_____

_____

_____

_____

_____

_____

_____

DAY 5   Luke 1:19

19 The angel said to him, "I am Gabriel. I stand in the presence of God, and I have been sent to speak to you and to tell you this good news.

MY HEART

Just like that ANGEL, we have been assigned to "share the good news" and that task is GOOD NEWS!

In Greek, Good News is also called The Gospel. The term Gospel is used 75 times in the New Testament. Christmas is about hearing, believing and RECEIVING the Good News of The Gospel. No other news trumps it! Not headlines or bank statements, not a doctor's diagnosis or an employer's bad report.

The GOOD NEWS, The Gospel, is so simple.

The virgin birth.

The coming of the Kingdom of God through His Son.

The death of Jesus on the Cross.

Jesus' resurrection to restore our relationship with God.

The Holy Spirit - a gift to believers.

The second coming of Christ.

Be like Gabriel! Shout the GOOD NEWS today!

Starbucks barista? Laundry clerk? Grocery cashier? Bus driver? Drug store attendant? Shout it aloud!

Prayer: Father, thank you for the simplicity of the Gospel. Thank you that I can simply receive it and I can simply share it. As we approach the Advent season help me to embrace the gift of an Unstuck Christmas. Help me to truly and intentionally keep you first and foremost in my mind and heart. Allow me to remember that you sent Jesus to be born to a sin-filled world in a musty barn and laid in a makeshift manger. I stand in your presence today, Lord. Speak to me. Speak through me. Amen

YOUR HEART

_____

_____

_____

_____

_____

_____

_____

_____

_____

_____

_____

_____

_____

_____

_____

_____

_____

_____

_____

_____

_____

_____

_____

_____

PAT LAYTON

_____

_____

_____

_____

_____

_____

_____

_____

_____

_____

_____

_____

_____

_____

_____

_____

_____

_____

_____

_____

_____

DAY 6   Luke 1:25 (NIV)

"The Lord has done this for me," she said.

My HEART

Honestly, this season of the year is such a gift. I realize as you read this (I am SEEING some of your faces in my head right now and smiling) that every Christmas is not the best. Sometimes the tough stuff of life messes up my "Merry." How about you?

You may have woken up this morning with critically ill family members, marriages in crisis (maybe even your own) and just plain heartbreak stains on your pillow. If not your own, simply turning on the news will do it.

So friend. Let's make a choice to OWN THIS DAY.

Let's make a choice to rejoice!

No matter what we see with our eyes or hear with our ears, let's echo the words of Elizabeth and make today about PRAISE! Let's declare together "what the Lord has done" for US! Let's keep this season as UNSTUCK as possible all the way to Christmas and beyond by filling our hearts, minds and mouths with a continuous list of God's love and goodness. Start by looking outside at the beauty of the world around us - a gift to be sure!

A simple sunset.

A glittering lake.

A huge puffy white cloud.

Breakfast. Lunch. Dinner.

A hot bath.

A cool drink of water.

Speak those blessings out loud and SAY, "This is what the Lord has done for me!" I would love to pray specifically for your need today.

Prayer: Father, you have done good things for me. I am thankful. Help me act like it. Amen

YOUR HEART

_____

_____

_____

_____

_____

_____

_____

_____

_____

_____

_____

_____

_____

_____

_____

_____

_____

_____

_____

_____

_____

_____

_____

DAY 7   Luke 1:28 (NIV)

The angel went to her and said, "Greetings, you who are highly favored! The Lord is with you."

MY HEART

Picture this: You are propped up on a narrow bed with pillows lifting your head and your feet snuggled firmly under your great-grandmother's heavy, crocheted blanket. Spicy hot tea steams from a thin china cup beside you and visions of sugarplums dance in your head as you are drawing the words "my wedding day" in swirly letters across the top of a crispy page of parchment.

This is really happening. You have seen the ketubah (marriage contract) signed by the required two witnesses. A flowing canopy of the finest silk snaps in the breeze around you, and visions of your beloved bring a slow smile to your face. You can almost hear the breaking glass and shouts of "Mazel tov" that will be the very first sounds confirming your soon coming transition from child to woman.

A mix of fear and excitement cause a shutter to travel from your toes to your head.

Suddenly, you are snatched from your sweet daydream by the deep melodic voice of a very large man who is standing above you dressed in the unrecognizable garments of a warrior. Something inside prompts you to run, but something deeper urges you to stillness.

The strange giant slowly raises his arm in a gesture of peace and speaks, "Greetings, you who are highly favored! The Lord is with you."

The parchment holding the childlike drawings of your dreams floats to the floor as you fall to your knees and the sound of breaking glass rings up from the teacup as it crashes to the floor and makes you a woman.

****

Honestly, I cannot personally imagine any words that could get a heart any more UNSTUCK than the words that Mary heard that fate-filled day.

To me, these words spoken by an Angel of the Lord, an Angel who stands in God's very living and Holy presence, shatter my heart.

"YOU are highly Favored."

"The Lord is with you."

Would it not be the highest imaginable honor?

So now let's reflect on some VERY good, UNSTUCK, news?

This is God's Holy Word.

This Word is for YOU!

This Word is for ME!

We, my sweet sister, are highly favored!

God is with us!

YES! YES! YES!

Write it on your hand, write it on a mirror, email to a friend! Instagram it! Dance to it. Cry to it. OWN IT!!

Prayer: Lord Jesus, you are mine and I am yours. You are my eternal Bridegroom and I am your beloved Bride. I am waiting for you and you are waiting for me. Unspoiled. Unbroken. Pure and forgiven. Fill me with your sweet presence today and I will be forever changed. Amen.

YOUR HEART

DAY 8   Luke 1:29-31 (NIV)

Mary was greatly troubled at his words and wondered what kind of greeting this might be. But the angel said to her, "Do not be afraid Mary, you have found favor with God. You will be with child and give birth to a son, and you are to give him the name Jesus."

MY HEART

Oh my. If we continue with our story from yesterday, we find a young woman, crumbled to the floor with shattered glass and the scent of sweet spices soaking into the rug beneath her knees. The deep-voiced proclamation that is still bouncing off the walls around her, is surely causing her head to spin. The fact that the New International Version of the Bible calls her "greatly troubled...and wondering..." is no great surprise. Who wouldn't be, right?

The New Living Translation calls her: 29 Confused and disturbed, Mary tried to think what the angel could mean.

The Message: 29-33 She was thoroughly shaken, wondering what was behind a greeting like that.

I ask you my friend, as we continue to think about this sister from generations past, can you relate? Has there been a time in your life when God said, did or allowed something to take place that left you "thoroughly shaken?"

As I write these words today, I am in more than one of those places. We have family and friends facing a thoroughly shaking health diagnosis, some experiencing the shatters of a divorce that should NOT be happening and many other "confusing and disturbing" life challenges.

When I think of these verses, I think of those moments of prayer and worship when I am overwhelmed by the tangible presence of God. Those moments fill my cup. Those moments keep me believing. Those moments give me strength when the ground is shifting beneath me and I cannot wrap my brain around what is happening or why.

My confident guess about this "Mary" moment in time is that the booming voice is the Angel Gabriel, whose name means "stands in the presence of God." While causing Mary's state of mind, he was at the very same time, the one who stirred her faith as a young, confused, disturbed, troubled and shaken woman.

For today, let's find a quiet moment to close our eyes, open our hearts and unfold our hands towards Heaven as we pray:

Prayer: I surrender my circumstances to you today. Make your presence known in my life and help me to walk the walk you have set before me with praise on my lips and faith in my heart. Help me overflow upon those around me with a special confidence that comes from you alone. Help me, Lord. Amen.

YOUR HEART

_____

_____

_____

_____

_____

_____

_____

_____

_____

_____

_____

_____

_____

_____

_____

_____

_____

_____

_____

_____

_____

_____

_____

_____

_____

_____

_____

_____

_____

DAY 9 Luke 1:32-33 (NIV)

32 He will be great and will be called the Son of the Most High. The Lord God will give him the throne of his father David, 33 and he will reign over Jacob's descendants forever; His kingdom will never end."

MY HEART

Today's verse truly sets the tone for our Christmas celebration and remains THE "Reason for the Season," as it's said. We have re-read and re-visited some familiar verses of the Bible over the past eight days. Likely nothing "new" to any of us but the thing that matters is that WE have chosen to stretch ourselves, to reach higher and dig deeper for a different kind of personal Christmas this year. I pray that you, like me, have found some fresh manna in God's word already. I have re-THUNK my thinking and remembered why I love this story and this season so very much.

The Angel Gabriel has our full attention at this point. I for one, have soaked up the greeting "highly favored" and "do not be afraid." Today as Gabriel continues his encounter with sweet Mary, his focus shifts from her state of mind and need for comfort to something, actually someone, far more important to the future of the world. I don't know about you, but I have OFTEN had to have that "come to Jesus meeting" myself.

Gabriel shifts from "you will" to "He will" in less time than it takes to say, "Merry Christmas!"

Gabriel makes a declaration that not only rocks Mary's world, but rocks the ENTIRE world.

"He will be great. He will be a King. He will rule FOREVER!"

If you have time for some extra reading, here is what I found in my research:

1. He will be great.

2. He will be called the Son of the Most High (cf. v. 76). The Septuagint often used the term "Most High" (hypsistou) to translate the Hebrew 'elyôn (cf. v. 76). Mary could not have missed the significance of that terminology. The fact that her Baby was to be called the "Son of the Most High" pointed to His equality with Yahweh. In Semitic thought, a son was a "carbon copy" of his father, and the phrase "son of" was often used to refer to one who possessed his "father's" qualities (e.g., the Heb. trans. "son of wickedness" in Ps. 89:22 [KJV] means a wicked person).

3. He will be given the throne of His father David. Jesus, as David's descendant, will sit on David's throne when He reigns in the Millennium (2 Sam. 7:16; Ps. 89:3-4, 28-29).

4. He will reign over the house of Jacob forever. Jesus' reign over the nation Israel as her King will begin in the Millennium and continue on into the eternal state.

5. His kingdom will never end. These promises must have immediately reminded Mary of the promise of Yahweh to David (2 Sam. 7:13-16). David understood the prophecy as referring not only to his immediate son (Solomon) who would build the temple, but also to the future Son who would rule forever. David stated that Yahweh had spoken of the distant future (2 Sam. 7:19). Mary would have understood that the angel was speaking to her of the Messiah who had been promised for so long.

Let's remember today friend that Jesus is GREAT!

Prayer: Lord, thank you for taking the time to comfort me as needed but also to shift my focus from my own fears and doubts to who YOU are what you promise. Father, remind me often as this day and upcoming weekend goes forward that you are GREAT!!

YOUR HEART

DAY 10   Luke 1:34 (NIV)

"How will this be," Mary asked the angel, "since I am a virgin?"

MY HEART

As I started writing today's devo and really began contemplating on this verse with a fresh heart (that's the goal here, right?), I started thinking about how the words of this verse might have left Mary with even more questions than she started with! I mean her "How will this happen" was answered with "the Holy Spirit will come upon you." Talk about answering a question with a bigger question.

Surely she was left wondering, "When he does come, will I know? Will he tell me when he is coming? Will he let me know ahead of time? What does he look like? How does that feel?"

I remember the first Christmas after I bowed my knees at an alter on June 9, 1984. I had always loved Christmas and all that it entailed, but that year was different. Quieter. Sweeter. Personal. I had laid my messy-self down at a physical alter and completely surrendered myself to Jesus. With a clear head and a humble heart, I knew exactly what the "Gospel" meant for the first time. I received Jesus as Lord of my life and I have never looked back. He has never abandoned His position in my life. I have wandered a little to the left or to the right but, praise His name, He has always been in eye view or arm's reach. He never leaves or forsakes us!

Today's verse and good news is, He is not afraid or offended by our questions, just as when Mary asked, not with doubt but with a sincere wondering, "HOW Lord? I am a virgin."

So friend, what is going on in your life today that prompts the question...."How Lord?"

Here are some tips I wrote down for myself:

1. Study God's Word for a promise that pertains to your need or question. Check your Bible concordance and see where all your need is mentioned.

2. Decide to believe what God says.

3. Journal/record your question and God's answers and state your faith as a prayer. Say it out loud so everywhere can hear.

4. Let God speak and change your heart.

5. Leave it with Him. He is able. If you find yourself carrying the question again, remind yourself that "God's Got This!" Imagine Mary walking away from Gabriel and living the details of the promise. Step by Step.

Prayer: Lord, you are amazing. You are good to me. In fact, you are GREAT! I trust you. I surrender to you. I look for your constant leading today, tomorrow and for as long as the questions loom ahead of me. I am thankful for the comfort of The Holy Spirit who walks with me through my questions and gives me the strength to believe. This is the day that you have made. I rejoice and believe!

YOUR HEART

_____

_____

_____

_____

_____

_____

_____

_____

_____

_____

_____

_____

_____

_____

_____

_____

_____

_____

_____

_____

_____

_____

_____

PAT LAYTON

DAY 11   LUKE 1:37 (NIV)

For nothing is impossible with God.

MY HEART

Hello friend—Happy Day #11

I continue to pray for you as we walk this journey together. I am honored by your friendship.

Today we are going to remind our heart who is in charge!!

We are going to order our words to line up with what we believe and know about God's good love.

Best of all, we are going to PLANT AND PLAN FOR A HARVEST!

Father, thank you that NOTHING is impossible for you. God, help me to trust, like young Mary did, in your sovereign plan regardless of its outcome. Help me to see you in every tiny detail and every single moment. Help me to be a blessing to those around me and to be your hands, feet and WORDS as I speak what ONLY YOU can place in my heart -faith, hope, trust, surrender, comfort. Truly, nothing is impossible. Read it. Think it. Talk it. Believe it!! Amen

YOUR HEART

Jot down an area where you need to hang on to some Mary kind of trust during this season!

DAY 12 Luke 1:38 (NIV)

"I am the Lord's servant," Mary answered. "May your word to me be fulfilled." Then the angel left her.

"Blessed is she who has believed that what the Lord has said to her will be accomplished!"

MY HEART

I have so many favorite verses in the Bible but this one is my FAVORITE, favorite!! This is my heart's desire.

This is who I want to be.

This is my mission statement, my vision and my assignment all rolled into five sweet words:

I. Am. The. Lord's. Servant. I - Me, Pat Layton. Wife. Mom. Daughter. Sister. Friend. Leader. Writer. Speaker. Decorator. Crafter. Cook. Housekeeper. Banker. Gift buyer. Gift wrapper. Hostess. Guest. Worshipper. Pray-er.... Me, Pat Layton.

I Am - Right now. Today. In this place. At this time. For these people.

I Am - Chosen. Assigned. Specific. Planned. Seen. Loved. Approved. Blessed. Challenged. Equipped. Anointed. Redeemed.

I Am the Lord's - Owned. Possessed. Captured.

Servant - Waiting. Obeying. Foot Soldiering. Honoring. Helping. Attending. Following. Shadowing.

I Am UNSTUCK by My Jesus, My Father God, My Holy Spirit.

Prayer: Father, THIS is the day that you have made. I rejoice in the season of celebrating your birth. I am thankful for who I am, who you have made me to be and what you have assigned me to experience, share, pass on, endure, learn and enjoy! I am your servant, Lord. Train me, lead me, show me your way. Amen

Now your turn. Make it personal.

I (your name)

Am (your situation today--Mom, friend, employee)

THE (specifically you--tired, excited, lonely, concerned)

LORD'S (who is Jesus to you today? provider? comforter?)

SERVANT (what is He asking of You?)

YOUR HEART

DAY 13   Luke 1:46-55 (NIV)

Mary's Song 46 And Mary said: "My soul glorifies the Lord 47 and my spirit rejoices in God my Savior, 48 for he has been mindful of the humble state of his servant. From now on all generations will call me blessed, 49 for the Mighty One has done great things for me holy is his name. 50 His mercy extends to those who fear him, from generation to generation. 51 He has performed mighty deeds with his arm; he has scattered those who are proud in their inmost thoughts. 52 He has brought down rulers from their thrones but has lifted up the humble. 53 He has filled the hungry with good things but has sent the rich away empty. 54 He has helped his servant Israel, remembering to be merciful 55 to Abraham and his descendants forever, just as he promised our ancestors."

MY HEART

Who we really are and what we really believe is squeezed out when we are under pressure. We can't hide it or fake it. When we are in trouble, afraid, threatened, or hurt, the abundance of our heart will overflow every time. In these verses, we see an example of a woman after God's own heart. We see why Mary has "favor" and why she is blessed. Mary fully believed that God would accomplish His purposes for her life, even in a time of trouble, fear, threat and heartbreak.

Every time I read through these words, I have to ask myself, "Is this how I would respond? Am I a woman who has positioned myself to receive all God has for me?"

You have seen this before but I know for a fact, you will love it again!

1. My soul glorifies the Lord and my spirit rejoices in God my Savior. A heart of praise

2. Mindful of the humble state of his servant. A heart of humility

3. Generations will call me blessed. A heart of confidence in which God designed His perfect plan for her life!

4. Mighty One has done great things for me-- holy is his name. A heart of gratitude

5. Lifted up the humble. He has filled the hungry with good things.

Prayer: Help me Lord, as the day of your birth and life is especially on my heart and mind—grow in me "a heart of surrender" Amen!

One of my favorite Christmas songs is playing in the background of my home.

"Mary, did you know that your baby boy would someday walk on water? Mary, did you know?

Let's break down Mary's song once more and embrace the overflow of a sold-out heart!

"His mercy extends...

He has performed great things...

He has (and will) brought down rulers from their thrones...

He has filled us with great things."

YOUR HEART

Write Your Own Love Song to Jesus!

_____

_____

_____

_____

_____

_____

_____

_____

_____

_____

_____

_____

_____

_____

_____

_____

_____

_____

_____

_____

_____

DAY 14   Luke 1:56 (NIV)

Mary stayed with Elizabeth for about three months and then returned home.

MY HEART

I'm thinking Mary desperately needed this time to be set apart, consider her situation, pray and ask God to show her the next steps, and to REST before what was surely to be a taxing assignment.

We are just a few days before Christmas and just days before the arrival of a brand-new year. I don't know about you, but finding "rest" before the birth of Jesus in our homes and hearts this year may not be an option. What I also know is that I am the only one who has the final say about MY "set apart" time. I have learned that it is fully up to me to make it happen, in whatever way my life and circumstances provide. This much I know: God WILL provide! He is good. He is able. He loves and cares for you and your well-being!

In the verses just before today's verse (Luke 1:46-55) we get a deep, deep look into Mary's heart. A heart that is filled with declarations about God's ability and character is a heart that pleases God and provides a place of rest.

Let's declare these truths today from the perspective of the REST and PEACE these promises should bring!

- God is mindful of the state of his servant (God is thinking about me)

- The mighty one has done great things for me (God has and will take care of me)

- His mercy extends to those who fear him (God is merciful towards me)

- His mercy extends from generation to generation (God is caring for my children, grandchildren, those I love)

- He has performed mighty deeds (God is able to take care of my messes)

- He has scattered the proud (God fights my battles)

- He lifts up the humble (God sees the desires of my heart)

- He fills the hungry with good things (God has a big plan for my life)

- He is our helper (God will help me do what I need to do)

- He keeps his word (God keeps His word!)

Mary had no idea about her future and did not understand God's plan for the salvation of the world through her unborn child. But, she did understand the character of God, as she beautifully proclaims in Mary's Song.

During this busy season remember Mary's Song, watch for His provision and rest in the faithfulness of our Savior.

Prayer: Lord, thank you that you are always mindful of my physical and spiritual needs. Help me find places, moments, and space for rest in this very busy time. Might you open a small slot for a cup of eggnog and a few minutes with my Unstuck Christmas and my journal? Thank you, Lord, for this season, so rich in your comfort and love! Amen.

YOUR HEART

_____

_____

_____

_____

_____

_____

_____

_____

_____

_____

_____

_____

_____

_____

_____

_____

_____

_____

_____

_____

_____

_____

_____

DAY 15   Luke 1:57-58 (NIV)

57 When it was time for Elizabeth to have her baby, she gave birth to a son. 58 Her neighbors and relatives heard that the Lord had shown her great mercy, and they shared her joy.

MY HEART

The following devotional was written by one of my "Besties." We are a small group of women, five to be exact. Although we each have many other close friends who pray with us, do life with us and walk out our highs and lows, this little group is special to each of us. We have been meeting together for as long as 26 years!!! Some have been in our little prayer group longer than others. The lovely lady that wrote this devotional, Jayne, and I were the original "Besties." The story of how we met is too long to tell, but such a goodie! Someday I will share it.

Anyway, my "Besties" are there for me and I am there for them - anytime, anywhere, for any reason. It is truly CRITICAL for us to have sisters in Christ who are really, really our inner circle in order to stay UNSTUCK.

Jesus set the example with His disciples and His three "Besties."

Here is Jayne's heart on today's verse:

I would imagine Elizabeth lived in a tight knit community where people worked together to accomplish the activities needed for daily living. Women most likely gathered at the well sharing stories and encouraging one another. Those who knew Elizabeth must have dropped their jaw in disbelief when she announced she was with child. This surprise would quickly turn to joy and these grown women most likely began hugging and jumping up and down, spilling their water jars. Shared joy is a gift. Do you have a group of women you gather with regularly? Perhaps this is in a Bible study, or in the break room at work. Consider your conversations. This Christmas season ask God to give you the gift of a joyful heart. Remind others of the Christmas miracle and share a miracle from your life. Sharing joy brings hope and sweeps away discouragement; joy connects us and softens our hearts.

Prayer: Lord, I am thankful to have faith friends who will share my joys and sorrows with me. I lift those up to you today and ask you to bless them, keep them strong. Hear their prayers, Lord, and show me how I might "share their joy" today. Amen.

NOTE: If you find yourself in a place today where those "Besties" of yours have drifted away due to busyness, location or even division, let your prayer today be for God to restore that empty place, to show you the way to some new like-minded friends who will share your joys and sorrows. We need one another.

YOUR HEART

_____

_____

_____

_____

_____

_____

_____

_____

_____

_____

_____

_____

_____

_____

_____

_____

_____

_____

_____

_____

_____

_____

_____

_____

DAY 16   Luke 1:59-61 (NIV)

59 On the eighth day they came to circumcise the child, and they were going to name him after his father Zechariah, 60 but his mother spoke up and said, "No! He is to be called John." 61 They said to her, "there is no one among your relatives who has that name."

MY HEART

"We always put the Christmas tree there."

"Our family always exchanges gifts on Christmas Eve."

"We always have......." "We always do...." "We never....."

Remember that old saying, "If you always do what you've always done, you will always get what you always got."

During this time period, it was Jewish custom to name the male child after his father or a close relative. However, in this case God wanted to do something DIFFERENT. It was His intention to set this child apart. The political and religious organizations during this time focused on legalism as the path to sanctification which was attained by compliance to rigid rules and laws. John would introduce the idea of grace found through repentance and acceptance of the Savior, Jesus Christ. Breaking tradition and cultural norms requires supernatural wisdom, courage and obedience.

As women, we strive for perfection, especially around this season. We desire to have our homes prepared for our families and guests. We spend time looking for the perfect gifts, wrapping and recipes. These are the expectations and traditions of the holidays. We accept exhaustion, frustration, and debt in order to participate in societal and commercial promotions, from now until the New Year.

This season we are getting UNSTUCK. We are asking God for the wisdom to examine traditions, expectations and cultural norms. It is God's desire that we begin the New Year with a renewed heart, a refreshed spirit, and a full cup of the Holy Spirit! Let's pray for supernatural wisdom, courage and obedience this season. These were the qualities of Elizabeth's heart that birthed her son John and his message to prepare our hearts for the greatest gift ever given to all mankind, our Savior, Jesus Christ.

Prayer: Lord, I want to hear from YOU today. I don't break traditions just for the sake of breaking them, but I want to be UNSTUCK from anything that gets in the way of what you want to do in me and through me. Open my eyes, ears and heart to hear your voice and your directions for THIS Christmas season! Don't let me be STUCK in the past, help me step into the new with you! Amen.

YOUR HEART

_____

_____

_____

_____

_____

_____

_____

_____

_____

_____

_____

_____

_____

_____

_____

_____

_____

_____

_____

_____

_____

_____

_____

DAY 17   Luke 1:66 (NIV)

Everyone who heard this wondered about it, asking, what then is this child going to be? For the Lord's hand was with him.

MY HEART

When was the last time you felt a sense of wonderment? Wonderment is defined as a cause or occasion for wonder, a sense of astonishment, and a marvel. In this case, everyone is wondering and asking about Elizabeth's child. This child would be the incarnation of wonderment delivered to us from the hand of God. Our wonderful Savior would be delivered to Bethlehem by the Potter's hand. The Lord's hand would stay with him until the very end of his life when Jesus would commend his spirit to God the father and ascend into the heavens.

So, I ask again...

When was the last time you felt a sense of wonderment? What marvels you and leaves you with a sense of awe?

I remember when our daughter Julianna was born at 1.5 pounds and 22 weeks gestation. As we watched her fight for her life and win, we asked: "What then is this child going to be? The Lord's hand is surely with her."

Sometimes we get so accustomed to the marvels around us, we miss them. We become desensitized to everyday miracles in our lives.

Don't miss the wonder of this Christmas season. In fact, LOOK FOR IT!

Marvel at the fact that no two snowflakes are alike or the vibrant red of the poinsettia or the baby Jesus, born in a stable, nestled in a feeding trough. I bet that birthing center was a surprise to Mary! Even in such humble surroundings, wonder was present, and homage was brought to this newborn King.

Prayer: Lord, thank you for stirring a sense of WONDER in me as I wander through this particular journey to an Unstuck Christmas. Stir up any complacency in me and replace it with awe and anticipation! I love you, Lord. I lift my voice, my heart and my arms to you. You alone fill me with wonder. Amen.

YOUR HEART

_____

_____

_____

_____

_____

_____

_____

_____

_____

_____

_____

_____

_____

_____

_____

_____

_____

_____

_____

_____

_____

_____

_____

_____

_____

_____

PAT LAYTON

DAY 18   Luke 1:67-77 (NIV)

67 His father Zechariah was filled with the Holy Spirit and prophesied: 68 "Praise be to the Lord, the God of Israel, because he has come to his people and redeemed them. 69 He has raised up a horn[a] of salvation for us in the house of his servant David 70 (as he said through his holy prophets of long ago), 71 salvation from our enemies and from the hand of all who hate us- 72 to show mercy to our ancestors and to remember his holy covenant, 73 the oath he swore to our father Abraham: 74 to rescue us from the hand of our enemies, and to enable us to serve him without fear 75 in holiness and righteousness before him all our days. 76 And you, my child, will be called a prophet of the Most High; for you will go on before the Lord to prepare the way for him, 77 to give his people the knowledge of salvation through the forgiveness of their sins…

MY HEART

Let's SING A SONG today!

I remember the exact moment in my life when I "GOT IT."

June 9, 1984 at about 8:00 p.m. in the evening. It was the moment when I knew God was God and I was a hot mess in need of His grace! His answers are always better than my answers.

There are times in our lives when we, like Zechariah, finally get it. We announce what God has done and will continue to do in the midst of past circumstances we did not understand.

After years of praying to no avail, Zechariah and Elizabeth now have been blessed with a child. They finally understand God's plan in the waiting and Elizabeth's ascension out of disgrace (Luke 1:21-25). Zechariah narrates the revelation of God's plan for our savior in his song in Luke 1.

To have that "aha" moment! To rejoice in the realization that past hurts, disappointments, loss, poor choices, disobedience and even lukewarm faith, all end in a song of praise to God. God is always at least one step ahead of us, and in this case, future generations!

Zechariah was privileged to see the hand of God in his past, and in the struggle the Israelites had endured since God swore his oath to Abraham (72). All of this was in place before Zechariah was even born. The "aha" moment is a gift from the Holy Spirit. It is the ability to piece together events in our lives, and trust the promise that all things work together for good, from generation to generation.

Can you recall an "aha" moment in your life? Share it with us in "The Club!"

Prayer: Father, I never want to forget those moments in my life when, by your grace, I "got it." Thank you for this journey through your word that I might be reminded of those special times to sing your praise like Zechariah did. I pray that a song remains in my heart today - a song of thanksgiving, praise and peace. Your way is always better than I can imagine it might be! Amen.

YOUR HEART

_____

_____

_____

_____

_____

_____

_____

_____

_____

_____

_____

_____

_____

_____

_____

_____

_____

_____

_____

_____

_____

_____

DAY 19   Luke 1:78-79 (NIV)

78 because of the tender mercy of our God, by which the rising sun will come to us from heaven 79 to shine on those living in darkness and in the shadow of death, to guide our feet into the path of peace."

MY HEART

Most of my life I have lived just minutes from the powdery white sands of the Gulf of Mexico. Let me just tell you friend, sunsets are amazing everywhere but, in my opinion, there ain't nothin' like a sunset off the Gulf of Mexico.

When my Dad was alive, he used to debate with me about the beauty of the sunset verses the magnificence of the SUNRISE! I admit, I see one a lot more than the other!

Zachariah uses the magnificence of the sunrise as an analogy in his song, as he describes the rising sun (son) coming to us from heaven to shine on those living in darkness and in the shadow of death. Zachariah's son John has been created by God to deliver this message of hope. John will announce to the world that our lives can be filled with light, and the Divine is coming to us to guide our feet into the path of peace.

I have a challenge for us this Christmas season. Yep another one! LOL! Since this is to be an INTENTIONAL JOURNEY, let's intentionally select a morning to get up and watch the sunrise. EEKS, did I just say that?! Let's power through.

Sit still in the darkness and watch the light slowly dissipate the darkness as the sun rises into the sky. As we allow this vision to permeate our spirit and resonate with the messenger in us, let us feel empowered to provide those around us with the knowledge of salvation, and remain steadfast in the understanding that all sin can be forgiven through the tender mercy of our God.

Let's choose to show God's love and shine on those living in darkness. For those of us who have recently lost a loved one, we can take comfort in the sun (son) shining on those living in the shadow of death, that He will guide our feet into the path of peace.

Prayer: Lord, as the sun rises I quiet myself to feel your warmth. There is someone I am missing today, Lord. Thank you for allowing the memory of loved ones passed to heal my heart. Help me to honor their life this season through acts of kindness, and celebration offered with them in mind. I acknowledge the majesty and the gift of the sunrise, so powerful to remove darkness from all the earth. Through its beauty I get a glimpse of the power of the risen Christ. Thank you for guiding my feet into the path of peace. Amen.

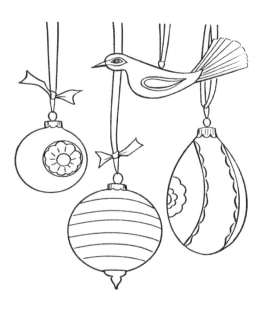

YOUR HEART

_____

_____

_____

_____

_____

_____

_____

_____

_____

_____

_____

_____

_____

_____

_____

_____

_____

_____

_____

_____

_____

_____

_____

_____

_____

_____

DAY 20   Luke 2:1-6 (NIV)

2 In those days Caesar Augustus issued a decree that a census should be taken of the entire Roman world. 2 (This was the first census that took place while[a] Quirinius was governor of Syria.) 3 And everyone went to their own town to register. 4 So Joseph also went up from the town of Nazareth in Galilee to Judea, to Bethlehem the town of David, because he belonged to the house and line of David. 5 He went there to register with Mary, who was pledged to be married to him and was expecting a child. 6 While they were there, the time came for the baby to be born,

MY HEART

Have you ever prayed for a parking spot to open just when you need it and it HAPPENS?! I always think of those silly times as a God kiss or even a giggle!

I recently had a crazy real-life moment where God's timing was absolutely tangible.

I won't go into the details but at the exact moment I was uttering a prayer for God's help and direction, the help and direction came. Now let me just say, I RARELY have the privilege of experiencing my timing match God's timing so specifically. In fact I am constantly seeking God's plan versus my plan!

God's timing is everything.

God's word is full of supernatural timing! It's not a coincidence that the call for a census was the first census that took place while Quirinius was governor at Syria (2:2). In fact it is very important to Dr. Luke that we recognize this fact. Once again, we see God's hand in fulfilling the Christmas prophecy. Timing.

The Old Testament tells us that a savior will be born to us in Bethlehem the town of David. Given the decree from Caesar Augustus, Joseph follows the law and he and Mary travel to Nazareth. He went to register Mary (Luke 2:5). Timing.

Now we have God's plan on paper, documentation for the future skeptic that requires evidence of this occasion. God left nothing to chance so that the more we investigate his words the deeper our faith becomes, just read, *Evidence that Demands a Verdict*, by Josh McDowell. Timing. Today's scripture sheds light on the faithfulness of God's promises.

What might be happening in your life, right now, today, that is a reflection of God's perfect timing? I can think of several. We have a choice every day to believe our actions are dictated by circumstances or directed by the Divine.

Prayer: Lord, I pray that in this season, I am sensitive to your perfect timing. I long for every move I make to be a step toward the greater plans you have for my life. I pray for obedience to your Holy Spirit promptings and a sensitive ear and heart to what you are directing me to do, say, complete. I trust your timing for fulfilling your great purpose in me.

YOUR HEART

_____

_____

_____

_____

_____

_____

_____

_____

_____

_____

_____

_____

_____

_____

_____

_____

_____

_____

_____

_____

_____

_____

_____

_____

PAT LAYTON

DAY 21 Luke 2:7 (NIV)

34 The angel answered, "The Holy Spirit will come on you, and the power of the Most High will overshadow you. 35 So the holy one to be born will be called the Son of God. Luke 1:34-35 (NIV) 7 and she gave birth to her firstborn, a son. She wrapped him in cloths and placed him in a manger, because there was no guest room available for them.

MY HEART

One of my favorite reads about the gifts of The Holy Spirit is *Forgotten God*, by Francis Chan. In my humble opinion, it is an amazing must-read for every Christian.

Here are a few excerpts from his book:

"...if the Holy Spirit moves, nothing can stop him. If he doesn't move, we will not produce genuine fruit-no matter how much effort or money we expend."

OK, how's that for a start??

What about this..."...when the Holy Spirit descended and indwelt the Disciples a radical change occurred. From that point on, none of these Disciples was ever the same. They were no longer timid or confused (remember the version we read about Mary); they were bold and inspired and began to declare and live the gospel of Jesus through the power of the Holy Spirit."

I want that, how about you?

Chan concludes his book with this basic, yet crucial fact:

"The Holy Spirit is God and therefore holy, eternal, all knowing, all powerful, fair and just."

I especially love Chan's list in the book of how the Holy Spirit shows up in our lives along with the Biblical references! If this was a book and not a five-minute devotional, I would share more about how the Holy Spirit has worked in my own life, but if YOU have some extra time today, do a bit of extra study on the Holy Spirit or maybe even gift yourself with this book! It's a life changer and a keeper!

Prayer: Holy Spirit, I stand in awe of you today. I do my best, with this finite mind of mine to understand and embrace your infinite, immeasurable, boundless love. I ask you, Holy Spirit, to come upon me in a fresh way today and give me power to live for Jesus and be more like him from the inside out. Inspire me, make me bold and, like Mary, overshadow my life in Jesus' name!

YOUR HEART

_____

_____

_____

_____

_____

_____

_____

_____

_____

_____

_____

_____

_____

_____

_____

_____

_____

_____

_____

_____

_____

_____

_____

_____

_____

_____

DAY 22   Luke 2:8-14

And there were shepherds living out in the fields nearby, keeping watch over their flocks at night. An angel of the Lord appeared to them and the glory of the Lord shone around them and they were terrified. But the angel said to them, "Do not be afraid I bring you good news of great joy that will be for all the people. Today in the town of David, a Savior has been born to you; he is Christ the Lord. This will be a sign to you: You will find a baby wrapped in cloths and lying in a manger.

Suddenly a great company of the heavenly host appeared with the angel, praising God and saying,

"Glory to God in the highest, on earth peace to men on whom his favor rest.

MY HEART

"Mom do you remember the first time you ever felt fear?" was the penetrating question posed by one of my children recently. He knew that fear has been a lifelong place of surrender in my life. The crazy thing was the minute he asked the question I remembered the exact event. My first memory of fear. God has led me through this healing journey for many, many years. It still grips me on occasion and I always revert to the pace he has told me to go. I take hold of the many promises I find in God's word to defeat it—again. Nighttime is my toughest battlefield.

I can imagine this scene. The shepherds sitting in the silence of the darkness knowing full well that enemies are lurking nearby, silently waiting for the perfect moment to attack. The shepherds were on alert. "Watching" the scripture says.

Waiting. Guard up. I can also imagine the sweet voice of God whispering—DO NOT BE AFRAID.

I am wondering friend—what is making you afraid today?

What assurance do you need from God to transition from fear to praise?

YOUR HEART

_____

_____

_____

_____

_____

_____

_____

_____

_____

_____

_____

_____

_____

_____

_____

_____

_____

_____

_____

_____

_____

_____

_____

_____

DAY 23   Luke 2:15-18 (NIV)

15 When the angels had left them and gone into heaven, the shepherds said to one another, "Let's go to Bethlehem and see this thing that has happened, which the Lord has told us about." 16 So they hurried off and found Mary and Joseph, and the baby, who was lying in the manger. 17 When they had seen him, they spread the word concerning what had been told them about this child, 18 and all who heard it were amazed at what the shepherds said to them.

MY HEART

This last part of the story regarding the birth of Christ asks two things of us.

First, like the shepherds, we should act on our faith.

After the angels had left them, the shepherds said, "Let us go to Bethlehem and see this thing that has happened which the Lord has told us about."

More importantly, they hurried off.

I don't know about you but I know for me, many mornings begin with good intentions to act out my faith, but all too often get delayed by circumstances and distractions. I love to consider how these shepherds were on a mission TOGETHER.

God said go, they went and, as a result, the word was spread concerning this child and all were amazed.

That is us. friends!

We have been and continue to be, on a mission together!

We are women of faith in action! We treasure God's promises in our hearts. We have made (and will have to keep making!) the choice to be unstuck and to:

1-Say to one another!

2-Act on our Faith

3-Spread the Word

4-Amaze the world around us. Our sphere of influence.

We are the right women, in the right place, at the right time! We are UNSTUCK!

Prayer: Oh Jesus, thank you for this journey. Thank you for these new friends. Thank you for connection and encouragement and hope. Thank you for your promise of tomorrow. Thank you for another Christmas to see you more clearly and love you more dearly. THIS IS A HOLY NIGHT! Amen.

YOUR HEART

_____

_____

_____

_____

_____

_____

_____

_____

_____

_____

_____

_____

_____

_____

_____

_____

_____

_____

_____

_____

_____

_____

_____

PAT LAYTON

_____
_____
_____
_____
_____
_____
_____
_____
_____
_____
_____
_____
_____
_____
_____
_____
_____
_____
_____
_____
_____

DAY 24   Luke 2:19 (NIV)

19 But Mary treasured up all these things and pondered them in her heart.

MY HEART

I am not, by nature, a "ponder-er" (probably no surprise there!) In fact, I am a bit too much of an "opinion-er;" a "fixer;" an "adviser." I want to be more like Mary. I want to be quiet and listen more. I want to hear God's still, modest voice. I want to pray and see what He does instead of pursue what I try to make happen on my own (THAT ONE is my weakest place.)

Here is my quick and stirring observation from my quiet time with Luke 2:19.

Mary was in touch with the "secret place" of her heart.

We have to intentionally "get to know" that quiet place where God speaks to us before we can actually practice and enjoy this experience. We have to CHOOSE Jesus over the world--every single day.

Over the past days and weeks we have focused on our personal "Inner Sanctuary." That place where we uncover and strengthen the joy of peace, faith, listening and waiting, and put aside the ever-pressing OUTSIDE world of strife, change, demands and needs.

I once heard this quote: "Ships cannot sink if storm waters stay outside, it is when the storm forces its way INSIDE that huge ships sink." The trick of the enemy is to flood our hearts with sin and unbelief. His best work is to get us to doubt the goodness of God, and in so doing, sink our ship. Remember Eve?

Mary pondered in her heart, her "secret place" INSIDE, what God had promised her and thus was able to trust and praise Him in the storm.

Glory to God in the Highest, and on earth peace to women- on whom His favor rests.

In His Grip with you!

YOUR HEART

_____

_____

_____

_____

_____

_____

_____

_____

_____

_____

_____

_____

_____

_____

_____

_____

_____

_____

_____

_____

_____

_____

_____

_____

_____

_____

DAY 25   Luke 2:20

The shepherds returned glorifying and praising God for all the things they had heard and seen, which were just as they had been told.

MY HEART

It's Christmas Day!! We did it!! LOL!

It is the LAST DAY (OH MY!) of this particular journey, but I know we will remain friends and hopefully explore another adventure together soon.

I would love it if you would visit me on any one or ALL of my social media platforms to continue what we have started in this Unstuck Christmas community. I'm looking forward to hearing your thoughts!

I close with these good words.

Ephesians 1:3 says you are blessed in Christ with every spiritual blessing in heavenly places. When you are secure in God's love, your presence is a joy to those who know you. From the deep well of your belonging and worth, you can bless others.

You are Blessed!

You Are Blessed to Be a Blessing.

Just like Mary, you, my friend, have been called, loved by God, kept by Jesus Christ and empowered by the Holy Spirit.

Let mercy, peace, and love be yours in abundance today.

Receive it! Take it all in and let it flow out!!

We find satisfaction in God's love ever more fully as we reach out to others from our own unstuck lives. From your wholeness, He will send you out to do all that He designed you to do. Share your life through encouragement, hope, and trust.

Pass on to others the passion to know Him.

From the overflow of your own heart, blessings spill!

Merry Christmas, darling friend, and Happy New Year!

My love and blessings, I hope to connect again soon!

Pat

Prayer: *Father, thank you that you have blessed my life in every way. Where I hurt, you comfort. Where I lack, you fill. Where I serve, you multiply. Where I wander, you lead. Where I stray, you chase. Where I dream, you open doors. Thank you that I am blessed today. Show me where I might be a blessing. Amen.*

NOTE: **I will be online in the Unstuck Woman Club the week between Christmas and the New Year to do some dream casting and new year planning!**

I have a FREE GIFT for you—

I hope you will join me there!

Visit patlayton.net

Please join Pat in the social media playground today for up-to-date happenings, including more information about speaking engagements, events, free gifts, products and MORE!

🌐 http://patlayton.net

ⓕ https://www.facebook.com/patlayton.author

⊙ https://www.instagram.com/patlayton

ⓔ https://twitter.com/patricialayton

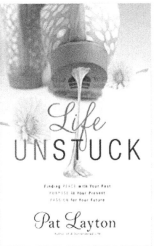

Join other women as we work our way from dizzy, desperate, and digging to a

Life Unstuck!

www.life-unstuck.com /

www.patlayton.net